Family Time Matters

Make it a Habit

21 Day Devotional

Jamytta Cheryl Bell

Family Time Matters Make it a Habit

TYRO Publishing Services
http://www.tyropublishing.com

Cover Design by Stefanie Miranda Designs

Unless otherwise noted, the bible quotations are from New International Version of The Holy Bible.

Printed in the United States of America

ISBN 10: 0986438561

ISBN 13: 978-0-9864385-6-1

Dedication

I am honored and humbled to dedicate to my loving, caring, supportive, blessed and blessing mother Eunice Evans, my first published daily devotional. If it is God's will, she will be receiving this book as her birthday present in 2015. I always ask myself "what do you give the mother that already has everything?" It quickly hit me to give her a part of me that I had not yet shared with her or anyone else. My mother has loved me unconditionally, supported me without question, and encouraged me to be who God has created me to be.

Foreword

"**F**amily Time Matters: Make it a Habit"

In the presence of the Lord is where I long to be and not without my family. To find ourselves with families living in the fifteenth year past the new millennium is an astonishing feat, according to our Christian predecessors. The longing to still feel connected to God, in the super-paced global world, must become a daily habit! God, our father, has never stopped looking for devotees. With all of the technology of this age, it cannot be more stressed that prophetically Jesus spoke concerning our present day in St. John 4:23, *Yet a time is coming and has now come when the true worshipers will worship the Father in the Spirit and in truth, for they are the kind of worshipers the Father seeks. NIV...*

Religious activity was disguised as worship for so long that it drowned out the validity of pure worship. Worshiping in prayer is a must in order to have a conversation that proves our devotion to our Maker. Then, worshippers have the neediness of his written Word to squelch out the collage of negative images that bombard the devoted believer's vision. Finally, a hymn or psalm of praise can only come from the heart, not from an 'app'. This daily devotional habit will move our family units, adjoining Jesus, navigator of your spirit, into the harmonious realm of the 'Higher Dimensions' of glory.

Regina Walden Alston, BS, MA, Mmin

Table of Contents

Introduction

It is amazing how those things that seem so minor make such a major difference in the family structure. I remember, as a child, when I was at my grandparent's house, not only was the food blessed by Grandpa Charlie, my great grandfather, Daddy Buddy, my grandfather, or Mama Nita, my grandmother, but everyone at the table said a Bible verse. Yes, that's right, EVERY ONE who could speak said a Bible Verse before we began to eat. Those meals were the best; not only because Mama Nita was the best cook for miles around, but because the presence of the Lord was truly in that house. "The Lord is my shepherd I shall not want" was not only spoken, but lived at 205 East Carter Street. No matter who came by the house during meal time, whether grown children, siblings, in laws, neighbors, doctor, pastor, or even strangers, the house never lacked anything at meal time.

My family like all other families had its share of challenges, yet I must say it was these fond memories that led me to want to write this family devotional. "Family Time Matters: Make It a Habit" is a collection of daily devotionals for families to do together. In the hustle and bustle of this 21st century in which we live, families rarely eat together, no least take the time to collectively and individually bless the meal. I invite you to take a few moments out of your daily schedule, perhaps meal time, but not necessarily so, and spend some QUALITY time with your family.

You know the old saying "The family that prays together stays together" but do you do it? Go ahead and try it for yourself. Indulge in this daily devotional with your family. It has been said that a practice can become a habit in 21 days. As you devote time you your family through this devotional during the next 21 days, you will see the importance of family time. Yes, "FAMILY TIME MATTERS: Make it a Habit.

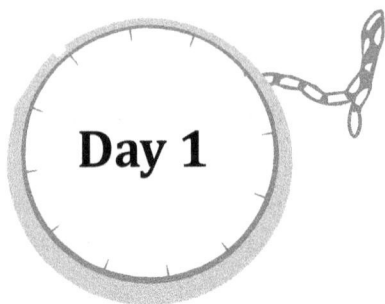

Day 1

Day by Day

Now is the Time

So do not worry, saying, 'What shall we eat?' or 'What shall we drink?' or 'What shall we wear?' For the pagans run after all these things, and your heavenly Creator knows that you need them. But seek first God's kingdom and its righteousness, and all these things will be given to you as well. Therefore do not worry about tomorrow, for tomorrow will worry about itself. Each day has enough trouble of its own.

Matthew 6:31-34

So often families do not see each other because everyone in the house who is of age to work, seemingly has to work in order to live a certain lifestyle. Yes, in order to live in a specific community, drive certain vehicles, and wear certain clothes, everyone must work, work, and work. Life seems to be full of all work and no play. Family members spend more time away from the home they are struggling to pay for than in the home with their loved ones. More hours are spent working to pay for the cars than time spent traveling with the family in the car. The nanny knows the children's habits and hobbies better than the parents. Why is this so? It is because everyone's desire for materialistic lifestyles is killing the firm foundation of the family structure. Take time today to plan a family day. Yes, pull out that technical gadget with your busy schedule and put your family on it. Stop worrying about the stuff and concern yourself with the blessings of family today. Do not look for an empty date on your calendar. Take the time to reschedule some other things. Family time matters so make your family first.

❄ Prayer ❄

Dear God, please give me the desire to make my family a priority in my life. As my family is a gift you have given me, let me take the time you have afforded me to be with them to share moments of love and laughter. As you have blessed us with many great gifts, let us realize that, next to your son, Jesus the Christ, our earthly family is the greatest gift of all.

Day 2

Just ask

"Truly I tell you, whatever you bind on earth will be bound in heaven, and whatever you loose on earth will be loosed in heaven. "Again, truly I tell you that if two of you on earth agree about anything they ask for, it will be done for them by my Father in heaven. For where two or three gather in my name, there am I with them."

Matthew 18:18-20

There are no perfect families. It is normal for things to go amuck in the family structure. Some family situations may be worst than others. However, there are no PERFECT families. There are no families that do not have some unhappy, irregular, abnormal, situations at some time or the other. Parents may argue, one or the other may have an affair; someone may lose his/her employment. Children may be disobedient in school, get in trouble with the law, and get addicted to drugs and in some cases a combination of all of the above. However, abnormality is not the end. When families dismiss the enemy, turn all matters over to God and bind the nonsense on earth, God will also bind the nonsense in Heaven. Take time today for you and your family to pray for God to be in the midst of what your family stands in need of, Health, deliverance, employment, promotion, unity, restoration. As you and your family gather together, know that God is in the midst of it all. Yes God is ready to work it out even if you cannot yet figure it out.

❄ Prayer ❄

Most Holy and everlasting eternal God, you know this family member by member. You created each of us in your image. Perhaps we have taken the free will given us and gone astray, yet today, we have come together asking you to put us on one accord and mend those parts which stand in need of repair. Dear Lord, as you see us individually and collectively, we ask in the precious name of Jesus that we will adhere to your Word, your will, your work, and your way. We are here together, we ask together, and we believe together. In Jesus name, Amen.

Day 3

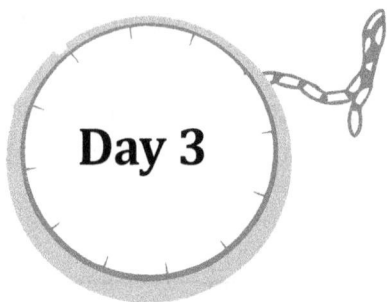

Greatest Plans

For I know the plans I have for you," declares the Lord, "plans to prosper you and not to harm you, plans to give you hope and a future. Then you will call on me and come and pray to me, and I will listen to you. You will seek me and find me when you seek me with all your heart.

Jeremiah 29:11-13

Do you remember playing hide and go seek as a little child? Do you remember running as fast and as far as you could hoping you would make it back to the safe space before you were caught and became it? As life went on and you became older, do you remember hoping to become it? You know, what I'm talking about. Do you recall having a crush and hoping to become his or her special someone, trying out for the sports team, hoping to make it and possibly even getting to be the coach, applying for a job, and praying to be the chosen candidate, having that good job, and hoping to get a promotion? Yes throughout life we all have plans. I'm sure as you take the time to reminisce some of these moments with your family; you may or may not be married to that first crush. You may or may not have made that ball team. Perhaps you got that job, got promoted, and have retired, or there is the possibility that you are presently on the job and often times are questioning why.

Whatever the situation is at the time, whatever condition your family status is in, remember God's plans for you are for you to have a future with hope. God plans for your entire family to have a grand future, yet your family needs to seek God in order to get the future God has planned for you.

❇ Prayer ❇

Dear God, we are aware that your plans for our lives are so much greater than our plans. Show us Lord how to be consistent in seeking you so that we will be recipients of the awesome plans you have established for us. As you order our steps and direct our paths Lord, let us walk in the fullness of God and accept the favor of God in every area of our lives.

Day 4

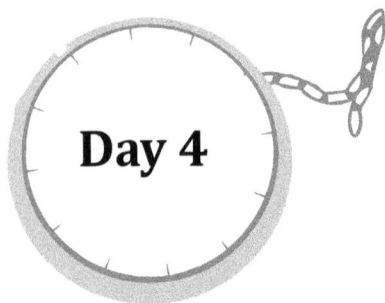

You Better Recognize

But you are a chosen people, a royal priesthood, a holy nation, God's special possession, that you may declare the praises of him who called you out of darkness into his wonderful light. Once you were not a people, but now you are the people of God; once you had not received mercy, but now you have received mercy.

1 Peter 2:9-10

It isn't about thinking you are better than others. It isn't about your family acting like they are better than the family across the street or even across town. No, it isn't about any of that. What it is about is your family recognizing who and whose they are. Once your family accepts the love of Jesus for them just as they are, they will desire to walk according to the word of God. It is imperative that the entire family recognizes that God has granted mercy. Matters of fact, God's mercies are new daily. No we are not perfect people, yet we are people serving a perfect God. On that note, recognize the crown you are blessed to wear. Show the world the Prince/Princess you are as a child of the true King of Kings.

❄ **Prayer** ❄

Lord, I know you know who I am. It is our prayer on this day that you show us individually and collectively who we are so that we will present ourselves to the world accordingly. Lord allows us to carry ourselves as the royal family you created us to be. Give us the heart, mind, and spirit to be royalty, for that is what you created and called us to be. In the precious name of Jesus we pray, Amen.

Day 5

And I know that

For you created my inmost being; you knit me together in my mother's womb. I praise you because I am fearfully and wonderfully made; your works are wonderful, I know that full well. My frame was not hidden from you when I was made in the secret place, when I was woven together in the depths of the earth. Your eyes saw my unformed body; all the days ordained for me were written in your book before one of them came to be. How precious to me are your thoughts, God! How vast is the sum of them!

Psalms 139:13c-17

We each were crafted in the image of God, yet we are each unique in our very own way. Look at your family. Yes, look at those present with you and visualize those who are living away, are perhaps on vacation, or maybe even those who have gone on before you. Yes, take the time to look at the family and then look at yourself. Wow, look at all of that greatness. Look at that vast measure of love, power, courage, humility, faith, respect and other characteristics that are seen through the heart and not with the eyes. It is not conceit, but your character, that allows you to proclaim you are fearfully and wonderfully made. It is taught in Genesis that everything that God made was good, therefore, that includes you. God, without doubt, without fear, without regret created you with all that the world needed from you. Go ahead and praise God for the gift that you and your family are to the world. Praise God for creating each of you in the image of God. Praise God because you and your family are fearfully and wonderfully made and you know that.

❆ Prayer ❆

Most gracious God, this is the day the Lord has made. We truly rejoice and are glad in it for you have blessed us just as we are to praise you once again. You have allowed us to praise you in spirit and in truth. Lord, as we are created in your image, we ask that you will equip us with that which we need to operate in your image as well. Let all that we do, be done as though we are doing it unto you. Because you have prepared a blessed life for us to live dear Lord, we ask that you will prepare us to receive all that you have prepared for us to receive.

Day 6

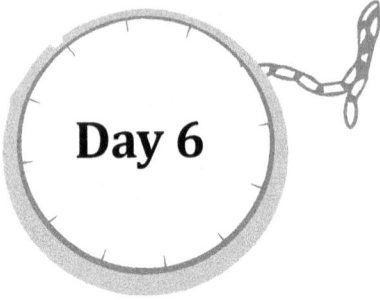

Stay Encouraged

Then Moses went out and spoke these words to all Israel: "I am now a hundred and twenty years old and I am no longer able to lead you. The Lord has said to me, 'You shall not cross the Jordan.' The Lord your God himself will cross over ahead of you. He will destroy these nations before you, and you will take possession of their land. Joshua also will cross over ahead of you, as the Lord said. And the Lord will do to them what he did to Sihon and Og, the kings of the Amorites, whom he destroyed along with their land. The Lord will deliver them to you, and you must do to them all that I have commanded you. Be strong and courageous. Do not be afraid or terrified because of them, for the Lord your God goes with you; he will never leave you nor forsake you." Then Moses summoned Joshua and said to him in the presence of all Israel, "Be strong and courageous, for you must go with this people into the land that the Lord swore to their ancestors to give them, and you must divide it among them as their inheritance. The Lord himself goes before you and will be with you; he will never leave you nor forsake you. Do not be afraid; do not be discouraged."

Deuteronomy 31:1-8

It is amazing how you can carry the torch for so long and yet there is so much more to do that you no longer have the strength to do. That is why God created family. From generation to generation, the knowledge and the strength shall move forward. The patriarch of the family may not be able to do everything as swiftly as he could in previous year. Each generation is to value every opportunity to sit at the feet of wisdom and gain knowledge and understanding of how things have been done, how to continue to do things better, and even how to do things new when it will make life better for the mass majority. Reinventing the wheel isn't always necessary, however, if a method other than rolling the wheel is found, by all means, allow the next generation, the youth, the youngsters, those taking up the rear to put it in place and make things happen. Just as God has been with our ancestors, with the past generation, with the older ones, know that God is also with the younger members of the family. Regardless of how things may look in this generation, just as God stayed with those of the past, God will remain with those of today as well. Keep every generation encouraged and reminded that God will never leave nor forsake them.

❋ Prayer ❋

Dear King of King and Lord of Lords, I ask that you will bless each generation of my family as we walk hand in hand with you. Dear Lord, please grant courage, wisdom, knowledge, and understanding as each generation of this family takes a stand and steps forward with God doing that which God has planned for us to do. Thank you most Holy God for being with us generation by generation. Eternally your child (every one say their name). In Jesus name we pray, Amen.

Day 7

Look up!

I lift up my eyes to the mountains—where does my help come from? My help comes from the Lord, the Maker of heaven and earth. He will not let your foot slip—he who watches over you will not slumber; indeed, he who watches over Israel will neither slumber nor sleep. The Lord watches over you—the Lord is your shade at your right hand; 6 the sun will not harm you by day, nor the moon by night. 7 The Lord will keep you from all harm—he will watch over your life; the Lord will watch over your coming and going both now and forevermore.

Psalm 121

You know how green the grass is on the past six lawns. You know what type shoes the past dozen or so people who walked by you have on. You can tell how many cracks are in the sidewalks on Main Street and how many times a dog owner didn't poop scoop while walking their dog. Yes, you know everything about everything that is down because you are on a constant journey with your head held down, yet you wander why nothing in your life seems to be going right. You must look up in order to get up. Your help comes from the Lord, and yes, although the

Lord sits high and looks low, nothing says God desires you to be constantly looking down or feeling down. As a family unit, each of you is called to encourage one another to look up.

God watches over your entire family, by day and by night. God desires to keep your family safe from all harm and danger. It is time for you to look up for God is truly ready to lift you up. You must look toward your help and not into your troubles. God's caring for you and your family is not a temporary gesture. No, God's caring for you is a permanent, eternal blessing.

❄ Prayer ❄

Most precious Lord, thank you for being omnipresent. How great it is to know that, wherever we have been, wherever we are, wherever we are going, yesterday, today, and forevermore we have been, are, and will continually be kept by you. Lord, when we are feeling down, lost, cast away by the world, and please give us the strength to look to the hills from where our help comes from. Lord, we know that we are forever kept by you for you never slumber nor sleep. We give you thanks this day for watching, blessing, and keeping us. In the precious name of Jesus we pray, Amen.

Day 8

Don't let Go

Let love and faithfulness never leave you; bind them around your neck, write them on the tablet of your heart. Then you will win favor and a good name in the sight of God and man.

Proverbs 3:3-4

It is so amazing to know that favor is available to us all. It may not always feel like we are walking in the favor of God and perhaps, based on our actions, sometimes we may not be. However, it is a blessing to know that when we do what God has instructed, we can receive the blessings of God. You do not have to physically wear a necklace that says "love" and "faithfulness", yet your behavior toward others should always show it. Your actions toward others will display what is in your heart. As a family, take the time to show each other that you love one another and are loyal to one another. Love and faithfulness are not bought but taught. It is necessary that each one in the family knows how to show love and loyalty to each other. Learn the love language of your family members and address them accordingly.

❄ **Prayer** ❄

Dear Lord, it is at this time, that we come to you asking that you strengthen our bond as a family. Please allow love to be ever present in all that we say and do, in every step we take, in all of our actions and deeds. Allow us to be loyal to you as you have shown your faithfulness to us throughout our lives.

Day 9

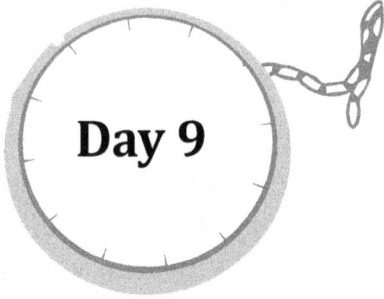

Even When You Don't Sneeze

If you fully obey the Lord your God and carefully follow all his commands I give you today, the Lord your God will set you high above all the nations on earth. All these blessings will come on you and accompany you if you obey the Lord your God: You will be blessed in the city and blessed in the country. The fruit of your womb will be blessed, and the crops of your land and the young of your livestock—the calves of your herds and the lambs of your flocks. Your basket and your kneading trough will be blessed. You will be blessed when you come in and blessed when you go out.

Deuteronomy 28:1-6

Has your family taken the time to recognize just how blessed you are? I mean to really recognize the blessing of one another. Perhaps it hasn't been recognized because it has not been verbalized. Family time matters, yet it isn't the quantity of time as much as it is the quality of time that creates the true blessing of family time. Take time to encourage one another to be and do the best in all things at all times. The power of family love is a blessing in itself. As a family realize you are always blessed, even when you do not sneeze, to have each other. Whether you are in New York, New York Big City of Dreams that never sleeps, or down in the fields where nothing can be finer than to wake up in North Carolina in the morning, know that God desires to bless you and your family. As a family, obey God, and just as God fulfilled the Word in scripture, God will bless you and your family as well.

❄ Prayer ❄

Dear God, we thank you for being such a blessing. We thank you for blessing us when we saw no way to simply make it through the next moment no least the rest of the day. Dear Lord, we give you thanks for allowing our family to be blessed in so many ways, but more than anything, we are blessed to have one another. Wherever we are, whatever we do, Lord we ask that you will continue to bless us so that we may be a blessing unto others. Amen.

Day 10

What are you waiting for?

May he give you the desire of your heart and make all your plans succeed.

Psalms 20:4

Nine days ago, on day 1, you were invited to schedule a date for your family. Do you remember that invitation? Have you taken the time to do it yet? If so, congratulations to you, I encourage you to begin planning your next outing. If you haven't done so as of yet, what are you waiting for? Tomorrow isn't promised to you. Go ahead, call your family, wherever they are, at least those who live at the same address, and tell them NOW IS THE TIME. Stop finding excuses: we cannot afford it, we do not have time, and we have nowhere to go around here. None of those excuses are acceptable on this day. If it is the desire of your heart to spend this special time with your family, whether you all are sitting home playing a board game, walking through the yard, counting the car lights that go by, simply spending the time together is important. Yes, family time matters and if it is a desire of your heart, God will surely bring it to fruition.

❄ **Prayer** ❄

Lord, grant us the time to spend with each other and value every moment. Let us dismiss all outside interferences. Do not let our minds focus on others or other things. Lord, allow us to stay focused on each other and recognize the value of who we are as a family.

Day 11

Step Up, Step Out, Step Away

David said to Saul, "Let no one lose heart on account of this Philistine; your servant will go and fight him." Saul replied, "You are not able to go out against this Philistine and fight him; you are only a young man, and he has been a warrior from his youth." But David said to Saul, "Your servant has been keeping his father's sheep. When a lion or a bear came and carried off a sheep from the flock, I went after it, struck it and rescued the sheep from its mouth. When it turned on me, I seized it by its hair, struck it and killed it. Your servant has killed both the lion and the bear; this uncircumcised Philistine will be like one of them, because he has defied the armies of the living God. The Lord who rescued me from the paw of the lion and the paw of the bear will rescue me from the hand of this Philistine."Saul said to David, "Go, and the Lord be with you." Then Saul dressed David in his own tunic. He put a coat of armor on him and a bronze helmet on his head. David fastened on his sword over the tunic and tried walking around, because he was not used to them. "I cannot go in these," he said to Saul, "because I am not used to them." So he took them off. Then he took his staff in his hand, chose five smooth stones from the stream, put them in the pouch of his shepherd's bag and, with his sling in his hand, approached the Philistine.

1 Samuel 17:32-40

You have been spending extra time with your family and the giant of all giants is truly upset about this. After all, when a family unites, there is so much power and strength available to them individually as well as collectively. The family can accomplish and overcome so much when they are all on one accord. Each member of the family has to do her/his part regardless of how small their part may seem. Step up to your family and let each person know you truly love and care about them and have their best interest at heart. Step out of your comfort zone and be willing to do what seems unexpected and out of the ordinary. Step away from nonsense, negative people, and chaotic situation. When the family comes together to take those three minor steps they will notice a major change in their family structure. The strengthening of the foundation requires each member to take their own step toward the rebuilding. Step by step, the family will grow.

❄ Prayer ❄

Dear God, there have been many giants, strongholds, challenges in our lives, yet because we know we can call and count on you, we pray for the strength to overcome and knock down each giant according to your teaching and guidance. Lord, we come believing you shall equip us as necessary, to go face to face with any giants that try to come up against us as we strive to live a life pleasing and acceptable unto you. As we go forth Lord, guide our hearts and our minds to go forth taking each step with God our creator, Jesus Christ the Son, and the empowering Holy Spirit.

Day 12

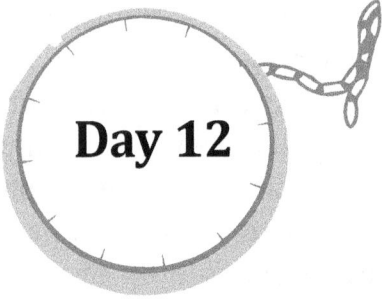

Tell me by showing me

This is how we know what love is: Jesus Christ laid down his life for us. And we ought to lay down our lives for our brothers and sisters. If anyone has material possessions and sees a brother or sister in need but has no pity on them, how can the love of God be in that person? Dear children, let us not love with words or speech but with actions and in truth.

1 John 3:16-18

Love, a word many say, yet have no idea of what it really means. Many say it to get someone to do what they want done. Some say it only after getting what they want from someone. Others say it just because it seems like the right thing to say. However, saying it isn't the command that was given. No. We were commanded to love, not simply to speak love. To do it, to show it, requires action. In order to love someone, will you seek to keep them from harm or danger, you will do your best not to cause them any harm or danger. Love, isn't a word or an action that should be reserved for holidays or special occasions. Love should be a natural characteristic that greets others before we open our mouths to say anything. Love can brighten a gloomy day, comfort a broken heart, and encourage.

Love your family before, during, and through difficult times. Often times showing someone that you really love them will make what seems like the most unbearable moment, bearable. Sharing and showing love shows that one is obedient to the Word of God.

❄ Prayer ❄

Most gracious God, please teach us how to love as a family. Teach this family to love even those who have hurt, betrayed, and deceived us. Teach us Lord not to harbor hatred in our hearts, yet to allow love to be the controlling action in our day to day lives. There may be times that showing love seems to be difficult we ask during those times Lord, that you will kill the way of the flesh and empower the way of the spirit, for we know the spirit has no dealings with that which is not of God and we know God is love. As we go forth day by day, we ask that we have the power to love throughout each day so that all who we greet can truly know they have been greeted with love.

Day 13

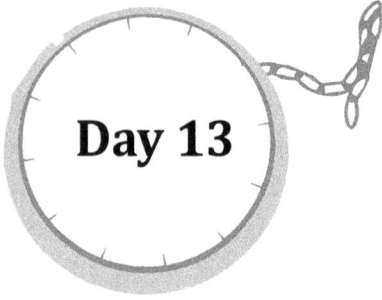

Walk in Expectancy

Consider it pure joy, my brothers and sisters, whenever you face trials of many kinds, because you know that the testing of your faith produces perseverance. Let perseverance finish its work so that you may be mature and complete, not lacking anything. If any of you lacks wisdom, you should ask God, who gives generously to all without finding fault, and it will be given to you. But when you ask, you must believe and not doubt, because the one who doubts is like a wave of the sea, blown and tossed by the wind. That person should not expect to receive anything from the Lord. Such a person is double-minded and unstable in all they do.

James 1:2-8

Life has a tendency to throw hard balls, fast balls, and sometimes curve balls. There are times when we may hit the ball out of the park and then there are the times we foul and sometimes we even strike out. I'm not speaking here of the ever popular baseball game. No, I am speaking of the trials that life sometimes pitches to us. Sometimes the trials seem to have a personal effect on one individual in the family. However, as family is connected, the secondary, emotional impact affects the entire family. For example, someone may be in school and having a challenge preparing for exams. Although only one individual is in class, the rest of the family is affected as well. The one trying to study needs peace and quiet yet other members of the household desire to watch television or play games. Or what about when one loses a job? The entire infrastructure of the family is affected. The budget is out of whack and everyone has to limit something(s) in order to make life bearable for all.

When you and your family find yourselves going through these trials and tribulations, don't let it get you down, beat you down, or weigh you down. No take the time to pray and praise through it all. That's right, in your weakest and worst moments, pray believing and praise expecting. Do not have a weak, wobbly, doubtful mind. That is the way of the non-believer. As you and your family go through to get to, know that God is with you every step of the journey. Do not approach your obstacles, challenges, heart breaking moments with fear and doubt. Walk in expectancy that God has prepared great things for you and your family.

❄ Prayer ❄

My God, my God, we call on you today to strengthen our minds. We ask whatever hardships we may face that you will bless us so that we can overcome. As we are experiencing the rough times, the disappointments, the negativity of this chaotic world, let us not forget that we are walking in expectancy of a mighty move of God. Let us keep our minds fixed on you, even during the worst of times. Lord, we know there will be moments where nothing seems possible, yet we shall not doubt for we know all things are possible because of you.

It is in your name that we pray, Amen, Amen, and Amen!

Day 14

Take off the Blinders and RUN to Your Blessing

So when it was evening on that day, the first day of the week, and when the doors were shut where the disciples were, for fear of the Jews, Jesus came and stood in their midst and said to them, "Peace be with you." And when He had said this, He showed them both His hands and His side. The disciples then rejoiced when they saw the Lord. So Jesus said to them again, "Peace be with you; as the Father has sent Me, I also send you." And when He had said this, He breathed on them and said to them, "Receive the Holy Spirit. "If you forgive the sins of any, their sins have been forgiven them; if you retain the sins of any, they have been retained." But Thomas, one of the twelve, called Didymus, was not with them when Jesus came. So the other disciples were saying to him, "We have seen the Lord!" But he said to them, "Unless I see in His hands the imprint of the nails, and put my finger into the place of the nails, and put my hand into His side, I will not believe." After eight days His disciples were again inside, and Thomas with them. Jesus came, the doors having been shut, and stood in their midst and said, "Peace be with you." Then He said to Thomas, "Reach here with your finger, and see My hands; and reach here your hand and put it into My side; and do not be unbelieving, but believing." Thomas answered and said to Him, "My Lord and my God!" Jesus said to him, "Because you have seen Me, have you believed? Blessed are they who did not see, and yet believed."

John 20:19-29

What will it take for you to really believe? Perhaps you have heard about the works of Jesus, yet like Thomas, you are waiting to see a miracle in your very own life. Have you seen many around you seemingly getting blessed over and over, time after time again, and everything pertaining to you and your family seems to be slacking and lacking? Are you having a spirit of doubt on the presence of God in your life because you cannot SEE any prosperity, any growth, anything positive going on? Do you doubt there is a move of God in your life because you haven't received what you asked for in your timing? Well, take a moment, sit back, and look over your life. Don't simply take a visual look, but take the time to let the happenings in your life roll through your memory bank. Allow the desires of your heart to become real. I guarantee you there have been times in your life that God moved so smoothly that you didn't even know it was God. You simply knew it wasn't you.

As long as you are depending on and believing in only what you can physically see, you will surely miss out on what God has for you. It is time for you and the entire family to see even in your darkest moments, that Jesus is the light. It is time for you and your family to receive your blessings based on what you believe in your heart according to the Word of God and not based on what you can see only with your eyes. As you take the time to focus on how much you truly need Jesus in your life, your eyes will be opened to how present Jesus has been and still is in your life. Take those blinders off that have had you going in the same direction over and over without, and let your visions run wild according to the work of God. Yes, believe even when you cannot see!

❄ **Prayer** ❄

Dear God, I know you know me. I know you have created a path for me to take. Where my belief waivers, Lord I ask that you will build me up and make a believer out of me. lord where I seem to have no focus, I ask that you will fix my focus on you. Lord, I ask the even if I lose my sight, that I will forever have my vision. Lord bless this family to believe in you for those things we cannot see. Thank you Lord for enhancing our spirit of belief so that we will continue to receive all that you have prepared for us.

In the precious name of Jesus we pray, Amen.

Day 15

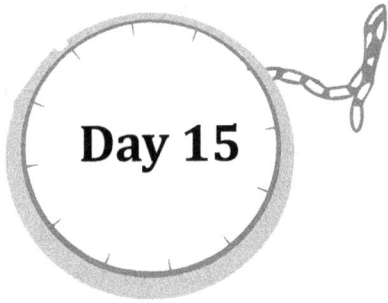

Try it For Yourself

Now during the day He was teaching in the temple, but at evening He would go out and spend the night on the mount that is called Olivet. And all the people would get up early in the morning to come to Him in the temple to listen to Him.

Luke 21:37-38

How you start your day can have a major impact on how you go through your day. How you go through the day can determine how you feel at day's end and how you end the day will determine how the next day begins. Your relationship with God should be continuous, never ending, one moment woven into, strengthening and building the next. Make sure you start each day early in the morning in conversation with God. Believe it or not, the best part of the conversation with God is when you take the time to hear from God.

❅ **Prayer** ❅

Dear God, thank you for allowing us to start each day with you. Thank you for going through each day with us. Regardless of any obstacles we may face each day, thank you for addressing those things we cannot address on our own. When the world tries to steal our happiness, we thank you for allowing us to forever have joy in your son Jesus. Thank you Lord for all things.

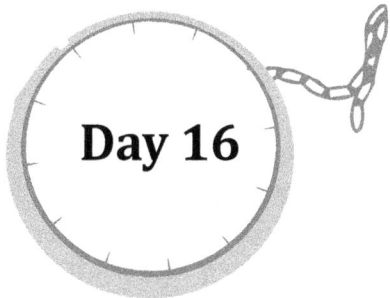

Day 16   Gold Medalist Training

The Spirit clearly says that in later times some will abandon the faith and follow deceiving spirits and things taught by demons. Such teachings come through hypocritical liars, whose consciences have been seared as with a hot iron. They forbid people to marry and order them to abstain from certain foods, which God created to be received with thanksgiving by those who believe and who know the truth. For everything God created is good, and nothing is to be rejected if it is received with thanksgiving, because it is consecrated by the word of God and prayer.

If you point these things out to the brothers and sisters, and you will be a good minister of Christ Jesus, nourished on the truths of the faith and of the good teaching that you have followed. Have nothing to do with godless myths and old wives' tales; rather, train yourself to be godly. For physical training is of some value, but godliness has value for all things, holding promise for both the present life and the life to come. This is a trustworthy saying that deserves full acceptance. That is why we labor and strive, because we have put our hope in the living God, who is the Savior of all people, and especially of those who believe.

Command and teach these things. Don't let anyone look down on you because you are young, but set an example for the believers in speech, in conduct, in love, in faith and in purity. Until I come, devote yourself to the public reading of Scripture, to preaching and to teaching. Do not neglect your gift, which was given you through prophecy when the body of elders laid their hands on you.

Be diligent in these matters; give yourself wholly to them, so that everyone may see your progress. Watch your life and doctrine closely. Persevere in them, because if you do, you will save both yourself and your hearers. If you point these things out to the brothers and sisters, you will be a good minister of Christ Jesus, nourished on the truths of the faith and of the good teaching that you have followed.

1 Timothy 4:1-16

As you gather for this time that you have set aside to spend with your family, please recognize that there are instructions here for the entire family present. Each one, regardless of how young or old, is afforded an opportunity to be active individually and collectively in the ministering of God's goodness. Each one can reach one. Each one should desire to reach one. Whether on the play ground, in the laundry room, or in the board room, God, Son, and Holy Spirit truly need be present. That presence should be found in you.

As you are preparing for the Gold Medal, it will not be for the physical training so much as for the spiritual training. Of course, physical training is needed to endure fulfilling the journey; however, the most important part of the journey is the building of, the spirit which will be strengthened by the relationship with the Trinity.

Do not give a portion of who you are. Give yourself totally so that your total progress can be seen. Do not be afraid to share The Trinity with others. Do not be afraid of telling others about the goodness of God and all God has done. Do not be afraid to speak up for justice and speak against injustice. No be bold enough to stand so that you can be a good minister of the mighty move of God available to all.

❄ Prayer ❄

Dear God, we seek your guidance as we stand to be bold ministers of your word. Regardless of what we seek to do, let us do it according to the Word of God. Whatever we do, whatever our age or gender, let that which is of you be received in a splendid way. Lord, let not our physical or spiritual age hinder us from telling others about who you are in my life. Let us go forth and continue to train for the only Gold Medal that will count the one we shall receive from you! Amen.

Day 17

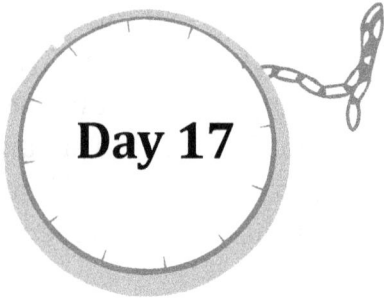

Because God said So

Now Moses was tending the flock of Jethro his father-in-law, the priest of Midian, and he led the flock to the far side of the wilderness and came to Horeb, the mountain of God. There the angel of the Lord appeared to him in flames of fire from within a bush. Moses saw that though the bush was on fire it did not burn up. So Moses thought, "I will go over and see this strange sight—why the bush does not burn up." When the Lord saw that he had gone over to look, God called to him from within the bush, "Moses! Moses!" And Moses said, "Here I am." "Do not come any closer," God said. "Take off your sandals, for the place where you are standing is holy ground." Then he said, "I am the God of your father, the God of Abraham, the God of Isaac and the God of Jacob." At this, Moses hid his face, because he was afraid to look at God. The Lord said, "I have indeed seen the misery of my people in Egypt. I have heard them crying out because of their slave drivers, and I am concerned about their suffering. So I have come down to rescue them from the hand of the Egyptians and to bring them up out of that land into a good and spacious land, a land flowing with milk and honey—the home of the Canaanites, Hittites, Amorites, Perizzites, Hivites and Jebusites. And now the cry of the Israelites has reached me, and I have seen the way the Egyptians are oppressing them. So now, go. I am sending you to Pharaoh to bring my people the Israelites out of Egypt." But Moses said to God, "Who am I that I should go to Pharaoh and bring the Israelites out of Egypt?" And God said, "I will be with you. And this will be the sign to you that it is I who have sent you: When you have brought the people out of Egypt, you will worship God on this mountain."

Exodus 3:1-12 | NIV

So often, children are told to do something they really do not want to do. They come up with a bunch of reasons/excuses why they cannot do it. They often give the excuses trying to get out of doing it, and will once they realize the excuses don't matter will ask, "Why do I have to do it?" This is why questions often anger parents. This is why many times questions are answered with the response, "Because I said so."

Today's scriptural reading shows us, how God was tried, tired and angered by Moses' responses to go and speak to Pharaoh. Please note that the anger of God can be much more difficult to bear than the anger of our parents. God has great plans for us and as our Heavenly parent; God will not ask anything of us that is not for our good. Do not be surprised at what God uses to get your attention. Do not be overwhelmed by what God may use as your "burning bush." Stay prepared as who you are in the family unit, along with the family unit as a whole, to know when God is seeking your attention in very unfamiliar manners. Know that God will do the least expected method by you to get the best expected results from you.

Whatever God create and calls you to do, know that God will be with you along the journey. Whatever your shortcomings are, God will send you one to fill the gap. Do not limit your greatness by focusing on what you cannot do. Accept the ordering of your steps by God and live without limitations.

❋ **Prayer** ❋

Holy, Holy, Holy, Lord God almighty, I ask that you will instill in me the ability to do, without limitation, WHATEVER it is you will have me to do. Dear Lord, WHATEVER method you use to get my attention, regardless of how senseless it may seem to me, please allow me to do it according to your will. Lord, I ask that you strengthen me so that when asked why I did what I did, my response will be "Because God said So!"

Day 18

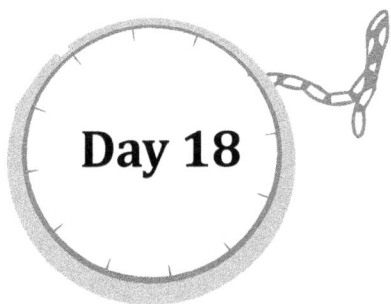

Call to Action

What good is it, my brothers and sisters, if someone claims to have faith but has no deeds? Can such faith save them? Suppose a brother or a sister is without clothes and daily food. If one of you says to them, "Go in peace; keep warm and well fed," but does nothing about their physical needs, what good is it? In the same way, faith by itself, if it is not accompanied by action, is dead. But someone will say, "You have faith; I have deeds." Show me your faith without deeds, and I will show you my faith by my deeds. You believe that there is one God. Good! Even the demons believe that— and shudder. You foolish person, do you want evidence that faith without deeds is useless? Was not our father Abraham considered righteous for what he did when he offered his son Isaac on the altar? You see that his faith and his actions were working together, and his faith was made complete by what he did. And the scripture was fulfilled that says, "Abraham believed God, and it was credited to him as righteousness," and he was called God's friend. You see that a person is considered righteous by what they do and not by faith alone. In the same way, was not even Rahab the prostitute considered righteous for what she did when she gave lodging to the spies and sent them off in a different direction? As the body without the spirit is dead, so faith without deeds is dead.

James 2:14-26

My, my, my, why is it that people expect results without action? Why do people have the tendency to put their beliefs on their religion, yet they have no relationship with the Divine? Your family has been called to action. It is time, perhaps past time, for some major changes to occur in your family. It is time for increase, healing, deliverance, overcoming, yet if you are simply believing God for it, and you aren't doing your part, the results will not be positive, the results will not be pleasing, the results will not be good nor Godly. The results will not be that which you were expecting of God. It will not be that God could not do it. It will not so much be a matter of you having weak faith, no it will simply be a matter of you being complacent and not doing your part. It is important that we always walk in expectancy of a miracle. The key is walking. Walking is an action verb. Walking requires movement. Walking requires us to do something. Therefore, take a look around your neighborhood and see where the needs are. Do not simply believe God can "fix things", see what you can do as a part of the solution. Homelessness, hunger, illiteracy, poverty, none of these are God's plan for God's people. On that note, respond to the call of action and partner it up with your faith and watch change happen. Are you asking what you are being called to do? Here are a few ideas: open a community food pantry with volunteers to help collect as well as distribute the foods where needed. Volunteer to read or listen to others read in schools. Keep a case of water in your car to give to individuals you see walking, bike riding, running because they have no other means of transport. Volunteer to take senior citizens to the grocery store or pick up their prescriptions from the drug store. Yes, your response to the call to action, with faith that God can fix it will bring forth a very powerful change as it builds a better community.

❊ **Prayer** ❊

Gracious, loving, precious Creator, I ask on this day that you will grant me with all that I need to respond however you call me. Lord I do know you do not stand in need of my help, yet it is my desire to work for you, every day of my life. Lord, please help me to help others so this world can be that which you created it to be. Amen

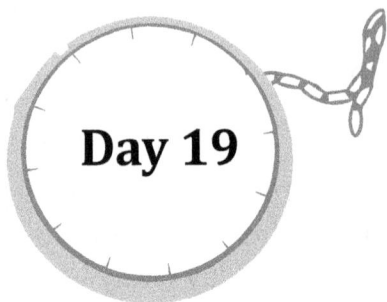

Day 19

Praise it Out

I will praise you, Lord, with all my heart; before the "gods" I will sing your praise. I will bow down toward your holy temple and will praise your name for your unfailing love and your faithfulness, for you have so exalted your solemn decree that it surpasses your fame. When I called, you answered me; you greatly emboldened me. May all the kings of the earth praise you, Lord, when they hear what you have decreed. May they sing of the ways of the Lord, for the glory of the Lord is great. Though the Lord is exalted, he looks kindly on the lowly; though lofty, he sees them from afar. Though I walk in the midst of trouble, you preserve my life. You stretch out your hand against the anger of my foes; with your right hand you save me. The Lord will vindicate me; your love, Lord, endures forever—do not abandon the works of your hands.

Psalms 138:-8 | NIV

Trouble doesn't last always, yet it is not prejudice. Trouble will come to every household. Trouble will tap you on your shoulder, kick your spouse in the behind, and go up beside your children's head. Oh yes, trouble has a way of creeping and sometimes boldly stepping into everyone's life at some time or the other. Well, aren't you glad to know that just as David stated in today's Psalm, we too can proclaim that God has preserved our lives. Yes, God has kept us from seen and unseen dangers. Those things we have been able to specifically thank God for is nothing compared to the many moments that would have claimed our lives a long time ago if it had not been for God serving as a preserver.

As a family, take the time to pray as well as praise God. As a family, recognize that God desires to serve as the head of your life and God deserves to serve as the head of your household. There is no good thing that God desires to keep from you. Praise is a great way to say thanks. Praise is the way to show that you know that not you, but God made all things possible. Praise is a way to move trouble out of your life.

As the children of the most high God, we are blessed because God keeps us daily and protects us against our enemies at all times. God will not abandon us, for we are truly the works of God's hands. Therefore, whatever your family may be going through, whether it is good or bad, just go ahead and Praise it Out.

❄ Prayer ❄

Most Holy and Everlasting Eternal God, as the author and the finisher of our faith, grant us the ability to praise you regardless of how we may find ourselves. Dear Lord, when trouble seems to invite itself into our lives, grant us the ability to praise it out. When those things that are not of you seem to want to take residence in our lives, give us the strength to praise it out. Dear God, we know as your children that life will still have its share of ups and downs, yet please let us stay focused on the fact that as long as we continue to look up to the hills from where our help comes from, that no matter how low things may seem, you will always reach down and pick us up. For that dear God, we are grateful for the opportunity to praise out troubles that are present as well as those that are lurking around the corner waiting to surprisingly attack us. It is in your name we pray, Amen.

Day 20

Grin and bear it

Even if I should choose to boast, I would not be a fool, because I would be speaking the truth. But I refrain, so no one will think more of me than is warranted by what I do or say, or because of these surpassingly great revelations. Therefore, in order to keep me from becoming conceited, I was given a thorn in my flesh, a messenger of Satan, to torment me. Three times I pleaded with the Lord to take it away from me. But he said to me, "My grace is sufficient for you, for my power is made perfect in weakness." Therefore I will boast all the more gladly about my weaknesses, so that Christ's power may rest on me. That is why, for Christ's sake, I delight in weaknesses, in insults, in hardships, in persecutions, in difficulties. For when I am weak, then I am strong.

2 Corinthians 12:6-10 | NIV

Oh yes, life is full of unexpected situations, moments that put us in shock. Some may be good and others not so good. Perhaps your family is going through or has been going through a situation that seems as though there is no end, no solution, no getting away from. Are you ready to throw in the towel? Is your spirit crying "enough is enough?" Well, just when you feel like giving up, God is ready for you to go down. You may need to go down to your knees, yet depending on the situation, you may need to go prostate, completely face down before the Lord.

You may not be happy with how things are going in your life right now, nevertheless, remember that during your weakest moments, God is your greatest strength. Through all your family may have gone through or may be going through, remember God's Grace is sufficient for all.

Go ahead and acknowledge God as King of kings and Lord of lords. As you recognize God for who God is, God will gladly show you just who God is. God's manifestation of greatness in your life is much greater than your subjection to the situations of your life.

❋ Prayer ❋

Gracious, loving, all wise God, we are so grateful for your being for us what we cannot be for ourselves. Lord we give much gratitude for your fresh grace and mercy every day. As we go forth in this day, individually, yet as a collective family, let us show the magnitude of how gracious we are for you being an omnipresent God. We know your blessings are always greater than our burdens, therefore keeps as we continue to keep our focus on you! In the precious name of Jesus, Amen.

Day 21

The Writings on the Wall

I will stand at my watch and station myself on the ramparts; I will look to see what he will say to me, and what answer I am to give to this complaint. The Lord's Answer Then the Lord replied: "Write down the revelation and make it plain on tablets so that a herald may run with it. For the revelation awaits an appointed time; it speaks of the end and will not prove false. Though it linger, wait for it; it will certainly come and will not delay.

Habakkuk 2:1-3 | NIV

One of the most difficult things for anyone to do is wait. Waiting is difficult, not because of what may happen, but because we do not always have an idea of what the end shall bring. As families, we wait for new births, family reunions, graduations, weddings, and other special events. These are normally all great events. However, every now and then the outcome is not what we were expecting. Upon completing educational requirements, many have intentions to move forward. Sadly, intentions are no good if there is no written plan. Therefore, I ask, what plans does your family have? Have you taken the time to sit still together and discuss a family plan for growth? Have you placed time in your schedules to stop and plan how to live a fruitful life? What vision have you created for your family to live a life pleasing and acceptable unto God as you do that which makes your heart flutter? Today's scripture teaches to write the vision and make it plain. Write it so that a herald may run with it. Exactly what does this mean? Well a herald is a fast paced runner. In order for the herald to get your vision it needs to be on point, direct, short and simple. Make the vision plain enough that not only you, but whoever sees it can understand and prayerfully sow into it. The most important part of your vision is to be sure that your vision lines up with God's will for, your life. As you and your family are creating the vision for your future, be sure that your vision board has GOD first!

❉ Prayer ❉

Gracious God, I give you thanks for blessing me with such an awesome family. As we have purposely, without regret spent the past 21 days studying your Word together, we have grown by leaps and bounds in our individual lives as well as a family. Dear Lord as we continue to intentionally spend time together, we ask that you will see our vision. We pray that you will be with us every step of the way as we do what you have called us to do and be who you have created us to be. With love and gratitude for your grace and mercy, as we are here together, let us say together Amen, Amen, Amen.

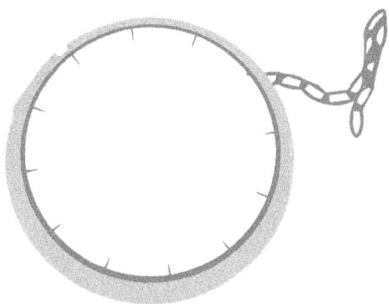

A Message from the Author

Rev. Jamytta Bell

To God be the GLORY. Your family should now be stronger, wiser, better equipped for the crazy, chaotic, nonsense that the world tries to put before you. There is strength in numbers.

It is my prayer that this first volume of Family Time Matters has given you a desire for more. It is my desire that your time together has allowed you to get to know self, each other, and God so much better. It is my prayer that every family which has participated in this devotional has grown closer in their walk with each other and closer in their relationship with the Trinity. Applaud yourself for completing the first 21 days of the rest of your life.

This is not the end of your family growth and change. This is only the beginning.

You are invited to order and incorporate Volume 2 of this series into your life. *Family Time Matters: Stay Connected,* should be available on line as well as in bookstores near you soon.

Thank you so very much for choosing to make a difference in your family.

www.ingramcontent.com/pod-product-compliance
Lightning Source LLC
Chambersburg PA
CBHW070032110426
42741CB00035B/2737